Prehistoric Creatures

Dinosaur Teeth and Beaks

Joanne Mattern
Reading consultant: Susan Nations, M.Ed., author/literacy coach/consultant

WR WEEKLY READER
EARLY LEARNING LIBRARY

M000101992

Please visit our web site at: **www.earlyliteracy.cc**
For a free color catalog describing Weekly Reader® Early Learning Library's
list of high-quality books, call 1-877-445-5824 (USA) or 1-800-387-3178 (Canada).
Weekly Reader® Early Learning Library's fax: (414) 336-0164.

Library of Congress Cataloging-in-Publication Data

Mattern, Joanne, 1963-
    Dinosaur teeth and beaks / Joanne Mattern.
       p. cm. — (Prehistoric creatures)
    Includes bibliographical references and index.
    ISBN 0-8368-4900-0 (lib. bdg.)
    ISBN 0-8368-4907-8 (softcover)
    1. Dinosaur—Juvenile literature. I. Title. II. Series.
QE861.5.M3483   2005
567.9—dc22   2005042869

This edition first published in 2006 by
Weekly Reader® Early Learning Library
A Member of the WRC Media Family of Companies
330 West Olive Street, Suite 100
Milwaukee, WI 53212 USA

Copyright © 2006 by Weekly Reader® Early Learning Library

Managing editor: Valerie J. Weber
Art direction and design: Tammy West

Illustrations: John Alston, Lisa Alderson, Dougal Dixon, Simon Mendez, Luis Rey

Printed in the United States of America

1 2 3 4 5 6 7 8 9 09 08 07 06 05

Long before there were people there were dinosaurs and other prehistoric creatures.

They roamed lands around the world. These creatures came in many shapes and sizes. Some had claws or sharp teeth. Others had spikes, long tails, or wings.

In this book, you will read about teeth and beaks. Look for a label with the creature's name. You will also see how to say its name.

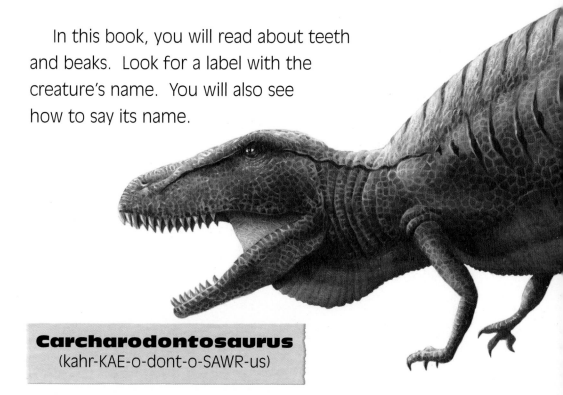

Carcharodontosaurus
(kahr-KAE-o-dont-o-SAWR-us)

Big Teeth

A dinosaur's teeth helped it catch and eat its food. Dinosaurs that ate meat had different teeth than dinosaurs that ate plants.

These big teeth belonged to a meat-eating dinosaur, or **carnivore**. The sharp points on its teeth were perfect for ripping into other creatures. From the size of its jaw, scientists think this dinosaur grew to be longer than two cars!

Megalosaurus
(MEG-ah-lo-SAWR-us)

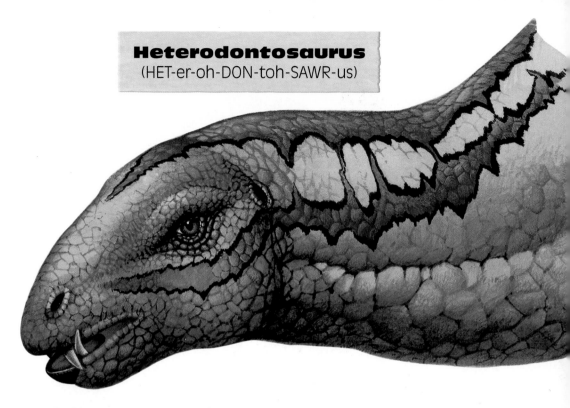

Three of a Kind

Scientists were surprised when they found this dinosaur's fossils. It had three different kinds of teeth! Its front teeth were long and sharp for ripping up plants. The back teeth were flat for grinding up tough leaves and stems.

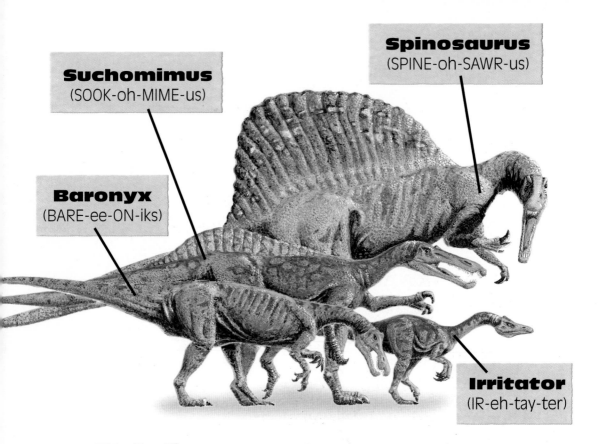

Suchomimus
(SOOK-oh-MIME-us)

Spinosaurus
(SPINE-oh-SAWR-us)

Baronyx
(BARE-ee-ON-iks)

Irritator
(IR-eh-tay-ter)

Fish Eaters

Some dinosaurs ate fish. These creatures' long jaws
held lots of small teeth. They probably grabbed
fish out of the water with their sharp claws. Then
they chewed them up with all those teeth!

King of the Dinosaurs?

This big dinosaur had long, sharp teeth. These teeth were just right for tearing into other animals. It could even grow new teeth if the old ones fell out!

The word *rex* in this dinosaur's name means "king." It is often called T. rex for short. Scientists used to think it was the fiercest dinosaur around. Now, however, they think these creatures might have eaten dead animals instead of hunting live ones.

Tyrannosaurus rex
(tye-RAN-oh-SAWR-us recks)

Shark Teeth

The big mouth of this dinosaur was filled with supersharp teeth! They were strong and curved like the teeth of a shark. Scientists think this big dinosaur was as long as the longest land animal today — the python snake!

Carcharodontosaurus
(kahr-KAE-o-dont-o-SAWR-us)

What a Mouthful!

Look at all the teeth in this sea creature's mouth! The shape of its mouth and teeth was just right for catching fish. This reptile's teeth also helped it hold tightly to its **prey**. An animal hunts and eats prey. Crocodiles have the same kind of teeth today.

Needle Teeth

This prehistoric reptile lived in fresh water. Its thin teeth looked like needles. The creature probably used these teeth to **filter**, or sift, tiny animals out of the water to eat.

Mesosaurus
(MESS-oh-SAWR-us)

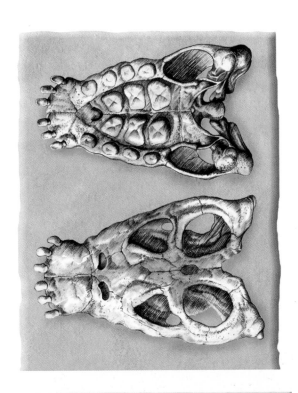

Placodus skulls
(PLAK-uh-dus)

All Kinds of Teeth

Its skull shows that this sea reptile had two different kinds of teeth. Its front teeth stuck out to pick up shells from the sea bottom. Its back teeth were strong and flat to crush the tough shells. Strong jaw muscles helped the animal bite down hard on its food.

Monster Teeth

This reptile looked like a real sea monster. It was longer than a tractor trailer. Its head alone was longer than a sports car. Sharp, pointed teeth filled this big creature's jaws. It swam through the oceans snapping up fish.

Kronosaurus
(KRONE-oh-SAWR-us)

Weird Teeth

Scientists are not sure how this sea reptile used its teeth. They stuck out so far that the animal would not have been able to catch fish with them. Maybe these creatures used their teeth to trap small fish in their mouths. Maybe they scraped the mud on the bottom of the sea to find food. What do you think?

What a Bite!

Tiny teeth that looked like needles filled this creature's jaws. These prehistoric reptiles ate smaller sea creatures. This one is about to snap up some tasty animals that look like squid. These were a favorite food of icthyosaurs.

Ichthyosaur
(IK-thee-oh-SAWR)

Teeth and Tusks

Long tusks stuck out of this sea mammal's mouth. Scientists think it used these big teeth to pull up seaweed or shellfish. The flat teeth in the back of its mouth crushed its food.

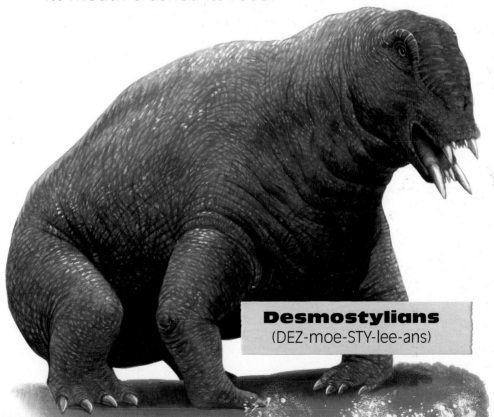

Desmostylians
(DEZ-moe-STY-lee-ans)

Dimorphodon
(die-MORF-oh-don)

Beaks and Teeth

This creature had both teeth and a beak! It used
its sharp teeth to grab and hold fish and other
prey. Its strong beak gave it a powerful bite.
Scientists think the beak was brightly colored
to signal other creatures.

Scissor Beak

This dinosaur's name means "ancient horned face." It also had a beak and teeth. Its jaws moved its beak like powerful scissors.

The teeth in its upper and lower jaws were different shapes. The pointed teeth on top helped grab plants. The flat lower teeth ground them up.

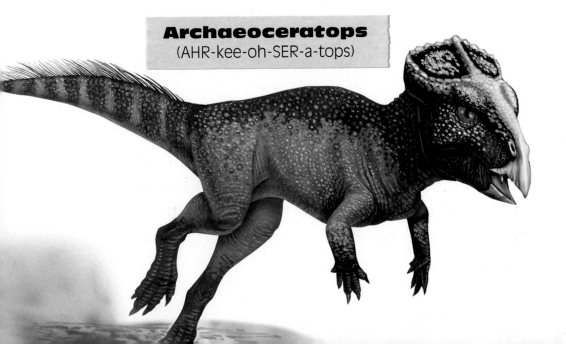

Archaeoceratops
(AHR-kee-oh-SER-a-tops)

Egg Eater

Scientists think this
dinosaur ate the eggs
of other dinosaurs.
It had a short beak.
Two bones on the roof
of its mouth tore the
eggs open as it swallowed
them. The dinosaur
could then get to
the tasty yolk and
baby animal inside.

Oviraptor
(OH-vih-RAP-tor)

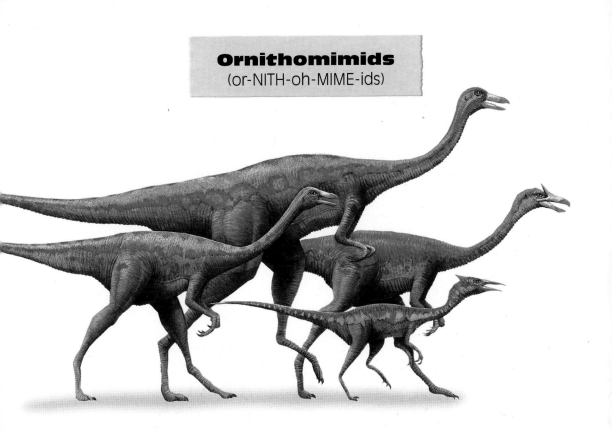

Not a Bird

These creatures looked like big birds, but they were all dinosaurs! They had beaks like birds and long legs with thick muscles at the top. Like some birds, they probably ate meat as well as fruit and leaves.

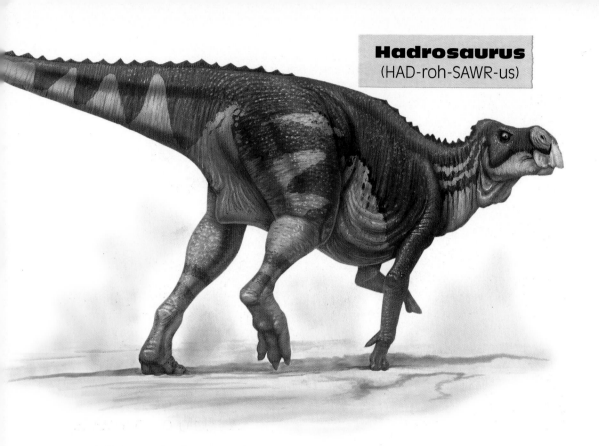

Duck Beak

This dinosaur's wide, flat beak looked like a duck's.
That's why dinosaurs in this group were called
duckbills. This creature was so heavy it had to walk
on four legs. It was an **herbivore**, or plant eater.

Different Teeth for Different Foods

Each of these flying animals had different teeth. Big, sharp teeth were good for catching lizards and other small animals. Small teeth or beaks could grab insects. Lots of thin teeth could hold slippery fish. A prehistoric animal's teeth or beak can tell us a lot about what it ate.

Pterodactylus
(ter-oh-DAK-til-us)

Glossary

ancient — very old

duckbills — a group of dinosaurs with mouths shaped like a duck's bill

filter — something that cleans liquids as they pass through it

fossils — remains of an animal or plant that lived millions of years ago

mammal — a warm-blooded animal that nurses its young

muscles — parts of the body that pull on bones to make them move

prehistoric — living in times before written history

prey — an animal that is hunted for food

reptile — cold-blooded animal with skin covered in scales or bony plates like armor

shellfish — sea creatures that have shells

skull — bones of the head that protect the brain

For More Information

Books

Pterodactyls. Dinosaur Series. Peter Murray (Smart Apple Media)

Spinosaurus. Discovering Dinosaurs (series). Daniel Cohen (Bridgestone Books)

Terrible Tyrannosaurs. Let's Read and Find Out Science 2 (series). Kathleen Weidner Zoehfeld (HarperTrophy)

Tyrannosaurus Rex: Fierce King of the Dinosaurs. I Like Dinosaurs! (series). Michael William Skrepnick (Enslow Elementary)

Web Sites

Smithsonian National Museum of Natural history
www.nmnh.si.edu/paleo/dino/jaws.htm
A tour of dinosaur teeth

Spinosaurus: Spiny Lizard
www.enchantedlearning.com/subjects/dinosaurs/dinos/ Spinosaurus.shtml
Diagram, facts, and a picture of this dinosaur to print out and color

Index

About the Author

Joanne Mattern is the author of more than 130 books for children. Her favorite subjects are animals, history, sports, and biographies. Joanne lives in New York State with her husband, three young daughters, and three crazy cats.